Advent
Bible Study
Series A
Study Guide

By Adam Francisco

CPH®
SAINT LOUIS

Edited by Thomas J. Doyle

This publication is available in braille and in large print for the visually impaired. Write to the Library for the Blind, 1333 S. Kirkwood Rd., St. Louis, MO 63122-7295; or call 1-800-433-3954.

Contents

About the Series

This course is one of six Advent-Lent adult Bible study courses. The Bible studies in the series are tied to the three-year lectionary. These studies give participants the opportunity to explore the Old Testament lesson, the Epistle lesson, and the Gospel lesson appointed for each Sunday during Advent and Lent.

Each course will draw you deeper into those parts of Scripture that deal with some of the greatest events in the life of Jesus—His incarnation and His passion. Although these courses may be used any time during the year, they were originally designed for the two most reflective seasons of the church year: Advent and Lent.

Each study is designed to help participants draw conclusions about each of the Bible lessons appointed for a Sunday, compare and contrast the lessons, discover a unifying theme in the lessons (if possible), and apply the theme to their lives. The Leaders Guide for each course provides additional textual information on appointed lessons, answers to the questions in the Study Guide, a suggested process for teaching the study, and devotional or worship activities tied to the theme.

May the Holy Spirit richly bless you as you study God's Word.

Session 1

The First Sunday in Advent

(Isaiah 2:1–5; Romans 13:11–14; Matthew 24:37–44)

Focus

Theme: Ready or Not

Law/Gospel Focus

We often find ourselves stumbling in the darkness of our sin, but God in the person of Jesus Christ has appeared to us in the midst of the darkness of our sinful condition. Through His incarnation, death on the cross, and resurrection from the grave, our evil deeds and sinful state are forgiven. We are given new life.

Objectives

By the enabling power of the Holy Spirit working through God's Word, we will

1. recognize that Christ's Second Coming is an imminent reality, but only God knows when it will happen;
2. look to Christ when we experience fear of the uncertain;
3. find hope and comfort through Word and Sacrament as we await the return of Christ.

Opening Worship

Sing or pray together as a litany the following stanzas of "Savior of the Nations, Come" (*LW* 13).

> Savior of the nations, come,
> Show Yourself the virgin's son.
> Marvel, heaven, wonder, earth,
> That our God chose such a birth.

No man's pow'r of mind or blood
But the Spirit of our God
Made the Word of God be flesh,
Woman's offspring, pure and fresh.

Father's equal, You will win
Vict'ries for us over sin.
Might eternal, make us whole;
Heal our ills of flesh and soul.

Glory to the Father sing,
Glory to the Son, our king,
Glory to the Spirit be
Now and through eternity.

Introduction

Constant drilling and preparation for possible conflicts are characteristic of a military service-member's life. Imagine that you are a submarine sailor. Your days and nights on patrol are filled with eager expectation. You never know what will happen next. It could be that you will be awakened from your sleep and expected to arrive at your work station within two minutes of the initial alarm. You never know whether the next alarm will be for a drill or the real thing. Your life is characterized by waiting expectantly for what may come next, always training and preparing for the unexpected.

1. What is it like to live in constant anticipation? How does the life of a submarine sailor help you understand your life as a Christian? Do you expectantly anticipate the return of Christ?

2. During the season of Advent, Christians prepare for the celebration of Christ's incarnation—the Word become flesh. We also look forward to Christ's Second Coming as we experience His daily coming to us by means of Word and Sacrament. How are you preparing for the events of the Second Coming? What can you do while you are waiting?

Inform

Isaiah 2:1–5 offers a glimpse of the end times. At the beginning of the passage in the second verse, Isaiah prophetically offers a promise—the Lord's temple would be established above all else. The temple was already esteemed, but at the end of time it will tower over everything. There will be no more need for instruments of war. War and evil will be brought to an end. Everlasting peace will abound, and God's love will be manifested to all so that all trusting in His promises will walk in His light.

Romans 13:11–14—St. Paul offers us hope in the promise of God. The hour of salvation (when we are brought into eternal life) is for all; it is a promise for all who trust in Christ. We are brought into the light and wakefulness through Christ who was given to die for us. We became part of the promise when we were clothed with Christ in our Baptism (Galatians 3:27). All those who are clothed with Christ and have participated in His death and resurrection are ready for the soon-approaching day.

Matthew 24:37–44 prepares us for the surprise of Christ's Second Coming through two analogies. In the analogy regarding the time of Noah, St. Matthew emphasizes the destruction that will accompany the Lord's coming. In the time of Noah, men saw the ark being built, but they disregarded God's warning even as it lay before them. Instead, they pursued their own fleshly desires. At the final moment of time there will be total destruction and man's blindness to God's incarnation will be his damnation. The picture of the men and women, one taken and the other left, is a picture of what happened at the time of Noah. The one being taken is symbolic of Noah; the one being left represents those who ignored Noah's warnings.

In the second analogy, Matthew refers to the surprise of Christ's Second Coming. He will come unexpectedly, like a thief in the night. The man in this short parable fell asleep, for he did not know when the thief would come. Jesus urges all to be ready; He will come when we don't expect it.

1. In the Gospel reading, what do the days of Noah and the short parable of the owner of the house teach us about Christ's return?

2. According to Matthew, how are we to be prepared for the Second Coming of Christ?

3. What does the Gospel reading say about those who try to calculate the time of Christ's Second Coming?

4. Do verses 40 and 41 of Matthew 24 imply that Christians will be taken from the earth while nonbelievers are left behind for a period of tribulation?

5. Paul writes in Romans 13:12, "The night is nearly over; the day is almost here." What do "night" and "day" allude to? How is the Christian life a life lived in the daytime?

6. What does Paul mean when he writes that we are clothed with the Lord Jesus Christ?

7. What outcome of Christ's return is pictured in the Old Testament reading?

8. What does it mean to "walk in the light of the Lord" (Isaiah 2:5)?

Connect

1. Scripture warns us to be ready for Christ's return. How did Jesus catch the people of His day off guard?

2. Why do you think so many people are concerned with the time of the Lord's Second Coming? What concerns do you have regarding Christ's return? How are you to be prepared?

3. Do you think that sin is more prevalent now than it was in St. Paul's time? What might you add to Paul's list of "deeds of darkness"? How might you or your congregation offer hope in a world filled with darkness?

4. What hope does Isaiah 2:1–5 offer to you? Read Matthew 21:1–22. How does this passage relate to Christ's Second Coming?

Vision

During This Week

1. As you prepare for the busy holiday season, take time to reflect upon and thank God for coming to you through the means of grace by which you are forgiven and prepared for the final judgment.

2. Think of ways you can bring the message of God's incarnation, death, and resurrection to those you come in contact with every day.

3. Look for opportunities to invite friends and family members to Advent services and Christmas services.

Closing Worship

Pray together:

Stir up, we implore You, Your power, O Lord, and come that by Your protection we may be rescued from the threatening perils of our sins and be saved by Your mighty deliverance; for You live and reign with the Father and the Holy Spirit, one God, now and forever. Amen.

Scripture Reading for Next Sunday

To prepare for the Second Sunday in Advent, read Isaiah 11:1–10; Romans 15:4–13; and Matthew 3:1–12.

Session 2

The Second Sunday in Advent

(Isaiah 11:1–10; Romans 15:4–13; Matthew 3:1–12)

Focus

Theme: *Rooted in Christ*

Law/Gospel Focus

God created man in His image. Adam and Eve's fall into sin and the sin we commit every day have destroyed that original divine image and severed our relationship with God the Father. Out of human and divine roots, God sent His Son in order to offer Himself as the final sacrifice for sin. Christ's death on the cross has restored people's relationship with their Creator and Father.

Objectives

By the enabling power of the Holy Spirit working through God's Word, we will
1. confess that we are sinful people from birth in desperate need of new life;
2. acknowledge God's eternal plan of salvation to come to us and remedy our condition on a cross;
3. wait patiently with expectant hope for Christ to return in order to bring us to eternal life.

Opening Worship

Speak responsively the Introit for this Sunday.
Leader: Restore us, O God;
Participants: Make Your face shine upon us that we may be saved.
Leader: Hear us, O Shepherd of Israel, You who lead Joseph like a flock;
Participants: You who sit enthroned between the cherubim.

Leader: You brought a vine out of Egypt;
Participants: And it took root and filled the land.
Leader: Restore us, O God Almighty;
Participants: Make Your face shine upon us that we may be saved.
All: Glory be to the Father and to the Son and to the Holy Spirit. As it was in the beginning, is now, and will be forever. Amen.
Leader: Restore us, O God;
Participants: Make Your face shine upon us that we may be saved.

Introduction

Scott and Bill spent the entire summer cutting down pepper trees in Bill's backyard. The trees hung over a steep embankment, so Scott and Bill had to labor especially slowly and carefully. After they had cut all the branches, they began to cut the trunks of the trees. They left a small portion of the trunk in the ground so that the roots would keep the soil from eroding. After several weeks of cutting and trimming, they decided to take a week-long break. When they returned to the backyard on a Monday morning, they found that the trunks had started to sprout branches with leaves. Bill turned to Scott and said, "There's a sermon here."

1. What do you think Bill was talking about?

2. Think of the times in your life when your faith was the strongest. What do you suppose caused it to grow?

3. It is easy to get caught up in a "Santa Claus Christmas." What do you plan to do in order to ensure that you and your family will remain firmly rooted in Christ over the holidays?

Inform

Isaiah 11:1–10—Isaiah offers a vision of peace. The "Root of Jesse" would offer peace with God to all who trust in Him for salvation. This "Root" would be Jesse's son, yet also be Jesse's root. He would be God in human flesh who would redeem His fallen creation and give them everlasting peace. Although the work of salvation was complete on the cross at Calvary, the Messiah will return to bring about the final judgment and humanity's earthly history will be finished.

Romans 15:4–13—God delights in the unity of His people. Just as Christ came for the Gentiles as well as the Jews, we are to accept all people as those for whom Christ died. The hope offered through the life, death, and resurrection of Jesus Christ gives all people a common bond. Paul makes note that it has been God's plan to raise up the "Root of Jesse" for all people. God promised this since the fall and restated His promises to the patriarchs until the time of Christ when the promise was fulfilled. The freedom won for us by Christ through His work on the cross fills us with "all joy and peace" as we trust in God's promise of salvation.

Matthew 3:1–12—The promised Messiah, who was to bring forgiveness to all who repent of their sins, had finally arrived. John was the one sent to announce His arrival as he echoed Isaiah's prophecy, "Prepare the way for the Lord, make straight paths for Him." John offered a warning to the Pharisees, Sadducees, and all people. All are to prepare for God's grace by acknowledging their sin. Our reception of God's grace does not depend on what group of people we belong to, but rather the gift of faith given to us through the Holy Spirit.

1. In Isaiah 11:1, what does the shoot that comes up "from the stump of Jesse" refer to? What does this say about the nature of the "shoot"?

2. What work would this "shoot" accomplish? What does verse 10 say about the effects of this work?

15

3. What is Paul speaking of in Romans 15:8 when he writes, "Christ has become a servant of the Jews . . . to confirm the promises made to the patriarchs"? How does this offer us hope?

4. In the Gospel reading, what is the significance of John the Baptist's words to the Pharisees and Sadducees: "And do not think you can say to yourselves, 'We have Abraham as our father' "?

5. What is the difference between John's baptism and the Baptism "with the Holy Spirit and with fire" described in Matthew 3:11?

Connect

1.a. Read Luke 3:23, 32, 38. Who was Adam's father? What does this tell you about the original state of humankind? Adam is humankind's representative. What happened after Adam sinned?

b. Who was Jesus' father? How is Jesus the second Adam?

2. Isaiah speaks of a coming Messiah who would have human roots, but would exhibit divine qualities. Why would the Messiah need to be both God and man?

3. Isaiah prophesies that Jesus "will stand as a banner for the

people; the nations will rally to Him." What past event in history stands as a banner for all people? What future event will stand as another banner for all people?

4. John the Baptist said, "The ax is already at the root of the trees." Without roots a tree will die. The further the roots are implanted in the ground, the healthier the tree will grow. When were you first rooted in Christ? How do you remain firmly planted in Christ?

Vision

During This Week

1. Think of ways you can raise the banner of Christ to those in your community, and follow through by planning an outreach activity.

2. The Lutheran dogmatician J. T. Mueller wrote in his book *Christian Dogmatics*, "The divine nature entered into a true and real union with the human nature, since the fullness of the Godhead dwells in Christ *bodily*." God came to earth in the person and work of Jesus and "gave proof of this to all men by raising Him from the dead" (Acts 17:31). No other religion claims that God became man. As you continue to prepare to celebrate the birth of Christ, ponder the surety of your faith found in the incarnation of Christ.

Closing Worship

Sing together the following stanzas of "On Jordan's Bank the Baptist's Cry" (*LW* 14).

> On Jordan's bank the Baptist's cry
> Announces that the Lord is nigh;
> Awake and hearken, for He brings
> Glad tidings of the King of kings!

Then cleansed be ev'ry life from sin;
Make straight the way for God within,
And let us all our hearts prepare
For Christ to come and enter there.

We hail You as our Savior, Lord,
Our refuge and our great reward;
Without Your grace we waste away
Like flow'rs that wither and decay.

Stretch forth Your hand, our health restore,
And make us rise to fall no more;
Oh, let Your face upon us shine
And fill the world with love divine.

All praise to You, eternal Son,
Whose advent has our freedom won,
Whom with the Father we adore,
And Holy Spirit, evermore.

Scripture Reading for Next Sunday

To prepare for the Third Sunday in Advent, read Isaiah 35:1–10; James 5:7–10; and Matthew 11:2–11.

Session 3

The Third Sunday in Advent

(Isaiah 35:1–10; James 5:7–10; Matthew 11:2–11)

Focus

Theme: The Remedy for Sin

Law/Gospel Focus

We are born spiritually dead on account of sin. We may try all sorts of ways to remedy our condition, but all attempts prove futile. God has seen our sickness and in response has sent the Great Physician to us. This Physician heals us by taking our sin and putting it to death with Him on the cross. Through His death and resurrection we are raised to new life with Him.

Objectives

By the enabling power of the Holy Spirit working through God's Word, we will

1. confess that we are terminally sick in sin, and in spite of our attempts to find a remedy, we are left lost in our sin;
2. look to Christ and His Word and Sacraments for forgiveness of our sin;
3. focus on our salvation, which came from God becoming man, dying on a cross, and rising from the dead.

Opening Worship

Sing or speak all four stanzas of "Hark the Glad Sound" (*LW* 29).

> Hark the glad sound! The Savior comes,
> The Savior promised long;
> Let ev'ry heart prepare a throne
> And ev'ry voice a song.
>
> He comes the pris'ners to release,
> In Satan's bondage held.

The gates of brass before Him burst,
The iron fetters yield.

He comes the broken heart to bind,
The bleeding soul to cure,
And with the treasures of His grace
To enrich the humble poor.

Our glad hosannas, Prince of Peace,
Your welcome shall proclaim,
And heav'n's eternal arches ring
With Your beloved name.

Introduction

Dolores had contracted the swine flu as a little girl. All the other children under the age of five on the seagoing trip from the Philippines to the United States had died, but miraculously Dolores's life was spared. She did suffer from one aftereffect of the virus: she was blind. As she got older, her faith began to waiver as she heard reports of miraculous healings going on in the church near her home congregation. She began to wonder why God hadn't heard her prayers and healed her. One Sunday she visited this church and asked someone to pray for her to receive sight. After praying for over an hour, she was told that she needed more faith in order for her to be made whole. At that moment Dolores remembered the words of the confession she had prayed for many years. The words were "We are by nature sinful and unclean." Dolores returned home and began to ponder what she had been told about her being made whole and what she had confessed at her home congregation for all those years. She began to thank God for what He had done in her life.

1. What do you think Dolores was thinking as she reflected on the confession, "[I am] by nature sinful and unclean"?

2. Do you think God could heal Dolores of her blindness? Is there a problem with the remark that her wholeness was dependent upon the amount of faith she had?

3. When had Dolores been made whole? When were you made whole?

Inform

Isaiah 35:1–10 begins by prophesying a day that Jerusalem would be freed from the Babylonian captivity. Isaiah points to an even greater event in the history of God's people. The promised Messiah would come, and He would make Himself known by opening the eyes of the blind and the ears of the deaf, by healing the lame, and by giving speech to the mute. This Divine Healer would be the one who would atone for the sins of the world through His life, death, and resurrection. This same Messiah will restore fallen creation in its entirety on the Last Day; the deserts will be glad and "the wilderness will rejoice and blossom" on account of God's work of redemption through His Son, Jesus Christ.

James 5:7–10 was written to Jewish Christians who had been scattered from Jerusalem all the way to Phoenicia, Cyprus, Syrian Antioch, and beyond (Acts 11:19). This dispersion was due to an outbreak of persecution following the stoning of Stephen. James offers comfort to the Jewish believers by reminding them of Christ's Second Coming. James illustrates their need for patience as they wait by alluding to a farmer who waits for rain to grow his crops. In James 5:11, Job is alluded to as an example of patience. In spite of all our trials and tribulations, we know, as Job knew, that our "Redeemer lives and that in the end He will stand upon the earth" (Job 19:25). Even after we have died, we will see God.

In Matthew 11:2–11 John the Baptist finds himself in prison under Herod Antipas. He begins to wonder if Jesus is really the one he had been waiting for. John sends his disciples to ask Jesus if He is the Messiah or if John should expect someone else. Jesus tells John's disciples to report that they have seen the sick being healed, the dead being raised, and Good News being preached to the poor. From this, it is clear to John that Jesus' ministry is a direct fulfillment of the prophecy from Isaiah 35:5–6. Jesus doesn't rebuke John for doubting, but affirms the importance of John's ministry to prepare the way for His coming.

1. Romans 8:22 says, "the whole creation has been groaning." Compare this to Isaiah 35:1–2. Both authors speak of creation, but in different ways. Compare and contrast the differences. What does this say about the work of Christ?

2. According to Isaiah, what are two things that will happen at Christ's Second Coming?

3. James 5:11 states, "We consider blessed those who have persevered. You have heard of Job's perseverance and have seen what the Lord finally brought about." Compare what you know of Job's life to the perseverance James is speaking of. Why do you think James used Job as an example?

4. In the Gospel reading, John the Baptist appears to be impatient as he sends his disciples to question Jesus, even though he had previously pointed to Jesus and said, "Look, the Lamb of God, who takes away the sin of the world" (John 1:29). Why do you think John the Baptist grows impatient? What evidence does Jesus offer John to verify that He is in fact the Messiah?

5. Even though John the Baptist questions whether Jesus is the Messiah, Jesus still speaks on John's behalf. What does Jesus say? What does this say to us when we experience impatience while waiting for the Lord's return?

Connect

1. Can you think of a time in which you were impatient with God? What was it that caused your impatience? During these times, what reminded you of God's promises?

2. James urges us to be patient and to keep from "grumbling against each other." James cites Job as an example. What New Testament figures can we look to for comfort in times of persecution? What are some ways you can keep yourself from grumbling against members of your congregation?

3. Isaiah 35:8 says, "A highway will be there; it will be called the Way of Holiness. The unclean will not journey on it; it will be for those who walk in that Way." Does this mean that we must be perfect in order to walk on this highway? Explain your answer.

Vision

During This Week

1. Christmas is coming soon. If you will spend time with friends and family over the holiday, think of ways in which you can share the message of Christmas—God's incarnation.

2. Along with your regular devotions for this week, review "The Sacrament of Holy Baptism" in Luther's Small Catechism.

Closing Worship

Pray together the Collect of the Day.

Almighty God, through John the Baptist, the forerunner of Christ, You once proclaimed salvation; now grant that we may know this salvation and serve You in holiness and righteousness all the days of our lives; through Jesus Christ, our Lord, who lives and reigns with You and the Holy Spirit, one God, now and forever. Amen.

Scripture Reading for Next Sunday

To prepare for the Fourth Sunday in Advent, read Isaiah 7:10–17; Romans 1:1–7; and Matthew 1:18–25.

Session 4

The Fourth Sunday in Advent

(Isaiah 7:10–17; Romans 1:1–7; Matthew 1:18–25)

Focus

Theme: *The Infinite in the Finite*

Law/Gospel Focus

God's original plan was that humanity would live eternally with our Creator. Through the fall of Adam, all people are born bound to sin and death on account of their sins. Christ came from eternity into a finite world, submitting Himself to God's Law. Through His sinless life, death on the cross, and resurrection from the dead, He substitutes His life for our lives. He gives us new life, life as God had originally intended—eternal life.

Objectives

By the enabling power of the Holy Spirit working through God's Word, we will

1. recognize that God's plan for humanity was that we would live eternally in fellowship with Him;
2. see the completion of His plan through the virgin birth of a child who would be "God with us";
3. rejoice in the mercy He has shown us through the death and resurrection of His Son.

Opening Worship

Sing together the following stanzas of "Oh, Come, Oh, Come, Emmanuel" (*LW* 31).

> Oh, come, oh, come, Emmanuel,
> And ransom captive Israel,
> That mourns in lonely exile here
> Until the Son of God appear.
> Rejoice! Rejoice! Emmanuel
> Shall come to you, O Israel!

Oh, come, oh, come, our Lord of might,
Who to Your tribes on Sinai's height
In ancient times gave holy law,
In cloud and majesty and awe.
Rejoice! Rejoice! Emmanuel
Shall come to you, O Israel!

Oh, come, O Rod of Jesse's stem,
From ev'ry foe deliver them
That trust Your mighty pow'r to save;
Bring them in vict'ry through the grave.
Rejoice! Rejoice! Emmanuel
Shall come to you, O Israel!

Introduction

Looking through your mail, you find an envelope that announces, "You are a winner!" There is one condition to receive your prize—you have to look at property someone is selling. You decide to go to collect your "fabulous prize." It turns out to be a fancy key chain. You're disappointed, but technically you are a winner.

1. What was the last big promise you were given? What were your initial reactions to that promise?

2. Have you ever heard a promise that you hoped would be kept, but it ended up being broken? Explain. What do you think of now when that person offers you a promise?

Thankfully, God has always kept His promises. Through His Son's death and resurrection, forgiveness is offered to all, even those who break promises. Today we will study the greatest promise ever given and the implications of that promise, which was fulfilled in the person and work of Christ.

Inform

Isaiah 7:10–17—God promises Ahaz and all people a sign that would change all of human history. "The virgin will be with child and will give birth to a son, and will call Him Immanuel." God tells Ahaz to ask for a sign that He would deliver the people of Judah. Ahaz wants things his way. He has already planned and appealed to the king of Assyria for help. He did not recognize that the Lord is in charge. God promises through the mouth of Isaiah that He is going to take care of the problem of evil once and for all through a virgin girl. This would be an unusual sign. This woman would give birth to a Son who would be both God and man. He would be the long-awaited Messiah who would deliver people from their sins.

Romans 1:1–7—Paul summarizes his ministry. Jesus, who had been foretold by the prophets, rose from the dead, further demonstrating that He was who He said He was. He called Paul to apostleship and sent Him to the Gentiles to preach the Gospel. Our calling is the same. We are to proclaim the Good News of Christ to all we meet. Paul reminds us that our faith is in the risen Lord Jesus who had been promised long before Paul's time. Through Jesus' death and resurrection we have received grace and mercy from God.

Matthew 1:18–25—Joseph is aware of Mary's pregnancy. At first, he plans to divorce Mary without anybody knowing what happened. Then an angel of the Lord appears to Joseph and speaks to him about the baby that is developing in Mary's womb. This baby is more than a child—He is God in human flesh. Joseph heeds the angel's instructions and marries Mary and gives the baby the name *Jesus*, which means "Yahweh (the Lord) saves."

1. In the Old Testament reading, how did Ahaz disobey the Lord? How did the Lord respond?

2. Some theologians and Bible translators have translated Isaiah 7:14 as "the *young woman* will be with child and will give birth to a son." What are the ramifications of substituting "young woman" for "virgin"?

3. What does Paul say is the evidence for Jesus being fully man while at the same time being fully God?

4. Paul was a Jew since birth and he knew the Old Testament Scriptures well. What does his statement "the Gospel promised beforehand through His prophets in the Holy Scriptures" say concerning the Old Testament?

5. In Matthew 1:18–25, compare Joseph's reaction to Mary's pregnancy before and after the angel of the Lord's appearance. What do you think about Joseph's character?

6. How does the New Testament reading connect with Isaiah's prophecy?

Connect

1. What does it mean to test the Lord? Is there anything wrong with testing the Lord? What do you think about asking our Lord for a sign?

2. In Romans 1:4, what does Paul use to defend Jesus' divinity? What hints might he give to you for evangelism and the defense of your faith?

Vision

During This Week

1. Review the Second Article of the Apostles' Creed and its explanation in Luther's Small Catechism.

2. Read the Gradual for this Sunday:

> Rejoice, greatly, O daughter of Zion!
> Shout, daughter of Jerusalem!
> See, your King comes to you,
> Righteousness and having salvation.
> Blessed is He who comes in the name of the Lord.
> From the house of the Lord we bless you.

In your devotions this week recite the Gradual in preparation for the celebration of Christ's coming for the redemption of all people. Remember to keep Christ's work and the consequences of His work central during the Christmas holiday.

Closing Worship

Speak responsively the Introit.

Leader: You heavens above, rain down righteousness; let the clouds shower it down.

Participants: Let the earth open wide, let salvation spring up.

Leader: The heavens declare the glory of God;

Participants: the skies proclaim the work of His hands.

Leader: In the heavens He has pitched a tent for the sun,

Participants: which is like a bridegroom coming forth from his pavilion, like a champion rejoicing to run his course.

Leader: It rises at one end of the heavens and makes its circuit to the other;

Participants: nothing is hidden from its heat.

All: Glory be to the Father and to the Son and to the Holy Spirit; as it was in the beginning, is now, and will be forever. Amen.

Leader: You heavens above, rain down righteousness; let the clouds shower it down.

Participants: Let the earth open wide, let salvation spring up.